NEATH & PORT TALBOT
Revisited

by David Roberts

**First published in Great Britain in 2017
by Bryngold Books Ltd.
100 Brynau Wood, Cimla,
Neath, South Wales SA11 3YQ.**

**Typesetting, layout,
editing and design
by Bryngold Books**

ISBN: 978-1-905900-48-0

Printed in Wales

www.bryngoldbooks.com

Neath & Port Talbot — two towns sharing one proud past

About the author

David Roberts has been producing pictorial nostalgia books focussed on locations around Swansea Bay for 20 years. The success of his first, featuring Swansea, resulted in a combined publication on the towns of Neath and Port Talbot.

This is the 19th in consecutive years on these two proud towns that the former South Wales Evening Post journalist has put together, each one as fascinating as those that have gone before.

David's books are unique in that they have offered residents of the communities they reflect the opportunity to involve themselves in the recording of their own history. Every aspect of daily life is included in his desire to ensure that we never forget the way we once were.

David Roberts

The publication of **Neath & Port Talbot Revisted** brings to a total of 40 his personal tally of books that all take his readers on an incredible trip back in time. His long running twin series has been widely saluted as an incomparable record of our lives.

Fresh and fascinating

The pages of **Neath & Port Talbot Revisted** provide a home for a fresh and fascinating harvest of images drawn from decades of picture taking in the two towns.

The book is a worthy companion to the previous titles in what has become a long-running series. With the rapid rate of change that these two important coastal locations are set to live with for many years to come, it will help ensure that the community will never have to look far to discover how things used to be.

The images depict much of the change that has occurred in the opening decades of the current century and indeed the one before. They are all important but in different ways and will no doubt bring memories flooding back for many.

The towns of Neath and Port Talbot both have a strong affinity with heavy industry, iron and steel making in particular, and at different times each has led the world. It is no surprise therefore that these industries provide their own crop of photographs. They don't always show the harshness of the working environment. Those who worked hard, played hard and this is reflected in the cameraderie evident in scenes of off-duty leisure moments where workmen became friends through their hobbies or over a pint. Such unity and togetherness is what these two towns have always been about, something that will continue to be so as the years march on.

Togetherness is also reflected in school groups, sporting teams or Whitsun processions. It is illustrated by families gathered in a park or on the beach; weddings too also spread the message and there are a number of these which also demonstrate a coming together within the community.

The faces change, the places change, but the heart of the community will always remain as the pictures revealed by each turn of a page in **Neath & Port Talbot Revisted** will testify.

**David Roberts,
2017.**

Appreciation

Neath and Port Talbot Revisited has only been made possible with the help and support of many people, not least all those who have shared and allowed the use of their memory-jerking images of people, places and events. These contributions, large and small, capture special times from the past and allow both towns to be seen from a different perspective, often through the eyes of those who were there, camera in hand.

I am grateful for the involvement of John Vivian Hughes, Hadrian Gower, Graham & Diane Gilbert, Jeff Thomas, Roger & Veronica Gale, John Newman, Bill Young, Audrey Walters, Peter Sodestrom, K Kingdom, John & Eira Beynon, Keith & Ann Davies, Vincent Thomas, John & Barbara Southard, Eileen Cottey, Robert Thomas, Anthony Taylor, Morris Fish, D Jones, Teresa Cummings, Helen Smith, Harry Humphries, Kester Reason, Robert Jones, Tony & Hilary Llewelyn, Carol Hancock, Derry Moore, Gaynor Gardner, Anita Care, Brian Harry, Margaret Bailey, Bill Adams, David Slee, Hilary Haines, Raymond Jones, Alan Williams, Clive Bowditch, Mervyn Roberts, Ray Griffiths, Eric Hill, Dominic & Tracy Davies, Harry Geil, Mark Collins, Val Thomas, Michael Hill, the South Wales Evening Post, Wendy Cross, Huw Thomas, Craig Wigley, Keith Borkett, Robert & Thelma Mason, Hugh Rees, Brian Selby, Colin Scott, David Robbins, Stephen Miles, Stephen Simons, Joan Powell, Stephen Pearce, Ray & Sandra Bruten, Jeff Bruten, Ann Joseph, Terry Hill, Pamela Davies, Stuart Davies, Colin Johns and David Beynon.

Others without whose help the book would not have appeared include Charlie Wise, Neil Melbourne and finally, I must thank my wife Cheryl for her unfailing support with every one of the books in this long-running series. Her behind the scenes involvement has, as always, been of invaluable assistance and not for one moment would I pretend that I could have done it without her.

Share your pictures

If you have photographs of people, places or events in and around Neath and Port Talbot right up to recent times then you could play a part in the next Neath and Port Talbot nostalgia book. Please telephone 01639 643961 or e-mail david.roberts@bryngoldbooks.com to discover the ways in which you can do this. All photographs, transparencies, negatives, black and white or colour, of people, places, events, streets, buildings, schooldays and sport are considered whatever their age, subject or format. They are all promptly returned. We can also receive your pictures electronically. Meanwhile, if you have missed any of the previous 18 books then please contact us as some titles are still available to help complete your collection. You can also check out our many other titles at:

www.bryngoldbooks.com

A youngster stands dwarfed by the facade of Margam Abbey, late 1950s.

Two perspectives of the Swing Bridge over the River Neath. Now permanently locked after the cessation of shipping to Neath Quay it was originally built to carry the former Rhondda and Swansea Bay Railway over the River Neath near Skewen. It is still used daily as a diversionary route running into the Swansea District line. The vessel on the left of the lower view is a former lightship moored just down river from the bridge.

Bakery store staff at the Aberafan Shopping Centre proudly display a cake baked to mark the visit of HRH Princess Anne to officially open the centre, 1975.

A group of sisters and cousins who were guests at a wedding in Cwmavon, July 1970.

Four Port Talbot men enjoy a few beers on a night out, early 1950s.

The driver of this former GWR class 56XX locomotive peeps from the cab as his goods train enters Briton Ferry goods yard and is about to pass under Shelone Road bridge, mid-1950s.

The Afan Lido Olympic size swimming pool, Aberavon Beach, mid-1970s and below, a view of the exterior of the building including its slide, shortly before its demolition in 2011 which resulted from a serious fire on the night of Wednesday, December 16, 2009.

Pupils of Form 1U, Llangatwg Lower Comprehensive School, 1982.

Visitors enjoying a stroll along the promenade at Aberavon during the one day NSA Afan Beach Festival, 2013.

Looking along Forge Road, Port Talbot, on a snowy day, 2013.

Valerie Hughes and BJ Hibbard in the booking office of bus and coach operator Thomas Bros. in Station Road, Port Talbot, mid-1950s.

Vehicles parked on the forecourt of Neath
General Railway Station, December 1974.

NEATH GENERAL STATION

A civic gathering at the Mayor's parlour, Port Talbot civic
centre on October 4, 1983 when representatives of the
2nd Port Talbot ..' Brigade Company presented Mayor of
the Borough of Afan, Councillor Raymond Morgan with
commemorative scrolls.

Children enjoy a traditional
Punch & Judy puppet show at the
annual NSA Afan Beach Festival
alongside the promenade at
Aberavon Beach, 2008.

Participants in the Neath 10K run, inside the Gnoll Rugby Ground, 1989.

Participants in Neath Carnival, with the Gnoll School and Fletchers car dealership just visible in the background 1979.

An array of pleasure craft lie in the mud at low tide in the River Afan, just below the lock gate entrance to Port Talbot Docks, February 2, 1995.

A teacher with her pupils at Catwg Primary School, 1973.

Participants in the 27th annual charity Boxing Day Dip organised by the Bay View Hotel, prepare for the start of the event at Aberavon Beach, 1998.

These four young policemen took part in a production of Oliver Twist, staged by pupils of Baglan Primary School, in the late 1970s.

Looking across Briton Ferry Ironworks and the back of Rock House alongside the top of the chimney on the far right, 1921.

Members of Port Talbot Amateur Operatic Society during a rehearsal for their production of
A Waltz Dream, 1979.

Remnants of the time when Cwmavon was an industrial powerhouse and behind, rows of local authority housing at Dan y Coed, 1967.

Pupils of Tonmawr Primary School with their teacher, on a visit to Ogmore Youth Camp, 1950.

A United Welsh bus company Bristol saloon with one of its double deckers behind, at Victoria Gardens bus station, Neath, early-1970s.

Demolition of retail properties in Water Street, Port Talbot, to make way for town centre redevelopment, late 1972.

The Port Talbot Hotel, Lower Water Street, mid-1960s.

Five senior pupils of Neath Boys' Grammar School who showed their prowess by becoming rugby internationals during the 1962-1963 season. In front of them are two proud members of the school's teaching staff.

Dismantling of the winding gear for refurbishment at Cefn Coed Colliery, Crynant. December 7, 2016.

Ruins of the Venallt Ironworks, Cwmgwrach, July 25, 1966.

Members of Cwmavon pensioners' group committee, 1981.

Thomas Bros. bus company employee Rennie Richards with conductress Thelma O'Callaghan and driver Harry Price alongside one of the company's Leyland Tiger Cub vehicles, late 1950s.

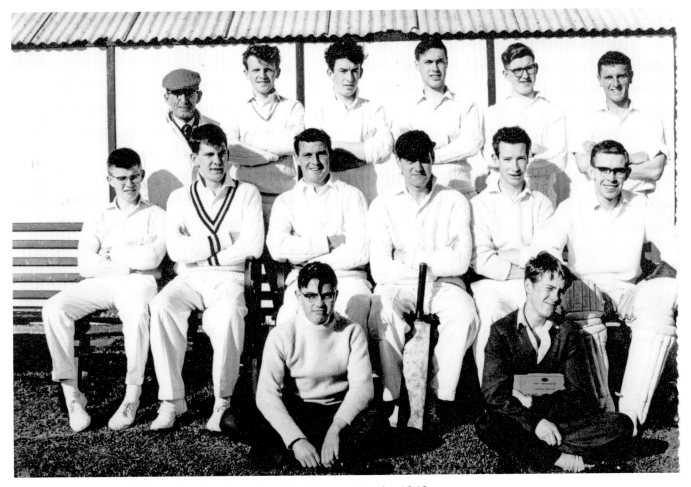
Members of Orchard Place Baptist Church cricket team, Neath, 1963.

Beulah Chapel, often referred to as the Round Chapel, Tollgate Park, Margam, early 1980s. It was dismantled and moved from its original site in nearby Groes village to facilitate construction of the M4 motorway.

Four instructors at the Metal Box factory, Neath, mid-1960s.

Some of the backstage crew of Port Talbot Amateur Operatic Society take a break during preparatory work for its staging of The Merry Widow, 1977.

The St Ives Inn, Church Place, Neath, 1984.

Chris Bridges gets the ball away during a Neath RFC game against Swansea, 1991.

Guests at a mid-1960s wedding at Sandfields, Port Talbot.

Members of the No. 4 Blast Furnace crew at the Abbey Works, Port Talbot, 1995.

Looking past The Harrier public house, The Parade, Neath, towards the town's castle, 1995.

Looking down on the Velindre district of Port Talbot and the Rutherglen depot of contractors Andrew Scott, from Lletty Harri, 1990. The depot has since been replaced by a housing development. The Ynys bowling green can also be seen.

The Bear public house, Penydre, Neath, 2006.

Allin the grocers at the junction of Wind Street and Water Street Neath, 1968. Much of the site is now occupied by the town's Boots the Chemist store.

A class of pupils of Blaenhonddan Primary School, Bryncoch, Neath, with their teacher, late 1960s.

The Mount, Taibach, early 1970s, with the Bell Inn in the background.

Some of those who took part in Anything Goes, the 2003 production of Port Talbot Amateur Operatic Society.

A class of pupils at Llangatwg Secondary School with their teacher and headteacher, 1960.

A South Wales Transport double decker bus heads along Orchard Street, Neath, at its junction with Alfred Street destined for Briton Ferry, 1950.

A group of employees watch the last tap of K Furnace at the Briton Ferry Steel Company Ltd., November 17, 1978.

Neath born mezzo-soprano, Katherine Jenkins OBE, enjoys some younger days fun on a tractor at Penstar Farm, Pontrhydyfen. 1988.

Traffic in Briton Ferry Road, at Stockham's Corner, Neath, July 1998.

Male chorus members of Port Talbot Amateur Operatic Society during a rehearsal for its production of the musical South Pacific, 1983.

1947-48

The locomotive shed of the Neath & Brecon Railway that stood some distance up line from Neath Riverside railway station, September 6, 1936. In the background is the former Vale of Neath brewery. Alongside is the Cadoxton Road depot of the Western Welsh bus company.

Members of the Central School team which won the Burton Cup after beating Velindre, during the 1947-48 season, seen with two of their teachers.

A brother and sister in the back garden of their home in Fairway, Sandfields, Port Talbot.

39

A locomotive hauls a train of empty coal wagons back up to one of the collieries at the head of the Afan Valley, early 1950s. Cwmavon is in the background, with the steeple of the village's All Saint's Church which was demolished in 1980, just visible on the left.

Construction of the Neath River bridge at Briton Ferry, early 1950s. Work on the project began in 1949 and was completed in October 1955.

A group of pupils at Catwg Primary School, Cadoxton, Neath, St David's Day, 1999.

Llangatwg Comprehensive School students head off to the school prom in a limousine, 2002. Included are Alex Beynon, Helen Morris, Katherine James, Amy Pritchard, Samantha Bowen, Georgine Kemble, Emma Williams and Ceri King.

A view across the rooftops of Briton Ferry during construction of the viaduct which was part of the Neath River Bridge scheme, early 1950s.

A group of pupils at Catwg Primary School, 1975.

Smoking stacks of Cwmavon Brickworks protrude through this view down the Afan Valley with the former Rhondda & Swansea Bay Railway line on the left, 1962.

The still, icy waters of the River Neath at low tide reflect a train heading out of Neath, January 1985.

Lord Snowdon and senior management representatives during a visit to BP Chemicals Baglan Bay plant after major expansion work, early 1970s.

Some of those who helped organise a party to celebrate the Coronation of Queen Elizabeth II, at Bryn, Port Talbot, 1953.

The school at Groes, Margam, mid-1930s. In the background is Beulah Chapel, often referred to as The Round Chapel. The village was levelled during construction of the M4 motorway.

Farmer Ray Bruten cutting silage using his Fordson Major tractor at Penstar Farm, Pontrydyfen, 1962.

The Britannia Inn, London Row, Cwmavon, before it was redeveloped into The Brit, 2013.

Aberavon Town railway station which served the former Rhondda & Swansea Bay Railway, early 1950s. The car park of the town's Tesco supermarket fills much of the foreground today.

Redevelopment work underway at Bridge Street, on the outskirts of Neath town centre, mid-1980s.

The British Aluminium works, Resolven, 1962.

First Minister Rhodri Morgan, Neath MP Peter Hain and Hospital Manager Karl Murray with Mrs Sandra Bruten of the radiography department at Neath Port Talbot hospital on February 3, 2003 the day it was officially opened by HRH The Prince of Wales.

A class of pupils at Central Junior School with their teacher and headteacher, late 1960s.

Two heavy duty machines shake loose the final section of the bridge that carried the road to Aberavon Beach from Aberavon over Afan Way, formerly the Rhondda and Swansea Bay railway line, May 2006.

The Neath and Tennant canal runs alongside the River Neath in this view downstream from the town's former road bridge, which linked the town with Cadoxton Road, mid-1980s.

Carmel Apostolic Church,
James Street, Neath, 1986.

Port Talbot Secondary School's hockey squad, with head teacher Gomer Rees and possibly the school's games mistress, 1947-48.

Looking eastwards across the Baglan Bay site of BP Chemicals, following expansion of the works, 1970. The last plant finally closed in 2004 and part of the site became home to Baglan Energy Park.

Looking down over the former
Metal Box factory, Penrhiwtyn,
Neath, 2010.

The owner of a preserved vintage tractor puts it through its paces at a carnival event in Neath.

Shops at Water Street, Aberavon which were later demolished to make way for town centre redevelopment, summer 1970.

A class of pupils at Dyffryn Comprehensive School, Port Talbot, mid-1960s.

One of the exhibitors at a popular stamp and coin fair held at Neath Town Hall.

A view over the Albion works of the
Briton Ferry Steel Company, 1977.

A September 1993 panorama of work on the M4 crossing of the River Neath at Briton Ferry.
The Ferryboat Inn is in the foreground.

With the stacks and towers of BP Chemicals' Baglan Bay plant in the background this picture offers a glimpse of work on the Swansea side of the river crossing, 1993.

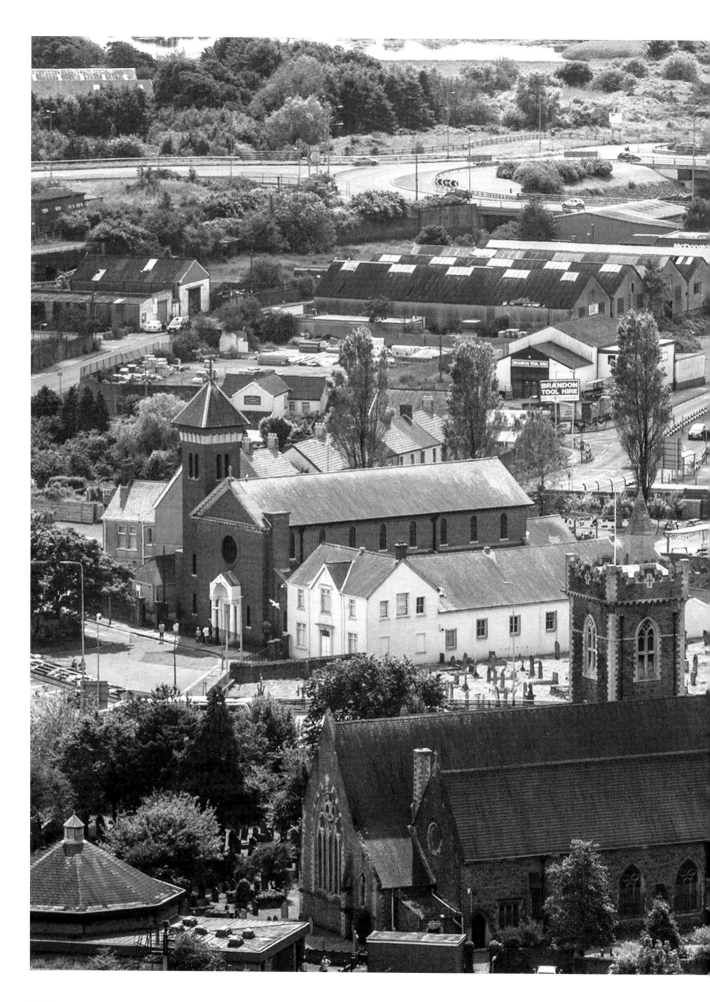

Looking seaward across
Port Talbot from the
mountainside, 2012.

A South Wales Transport 'Town Mini' bus at Victoria Gardens bus station, Neath all set for its next journey on route N3 to Ridgewood Gardens, Cimla, May 7, 1988.

The now demolished Sandfields Youth Centre, known locally as 'the youthy'. Gone to make way for the campus of Ysgol Bae Baglan, 2013.

Rich and Mary Bruten and their young son Jeff with the horse and cart that delivered milk for many years to much of the Pontrhydyfen area from Penstar Farm. The picture is believed to have been taken by the village's famous singing star Ivor Emmanuel in 1948.

Some of the younger pupils who attended Catwg Primary School, Cadoxton, 1974.

David John Daniels, caretaker of the County School (Glanafan) Port Talbot, proudly displays the trophy he won at the Llandrindod Wells bowls championship.

This couple, Mary Elizabeth Daniel and John Grantley Ridsdale were married at Ebenezer Chapel, Port Talbot in 1929.

This fascinating scene was captured near Neath Riverside railway Station in the early 1950s and shows both the Neath & Brecon Railway and the Vale of Neath Railway. The Vale of Neath brewery can be seen in the background to the left. The Vale of Neath business park occupies some of this land now.

Royal Buildings, Talbot Road, Port Talbot, before demolition, 2012. The site has since become home to a modern building consisting of flats and ground floor retail premises.

These seven young ladies were all members of Cadoxton Girl Guide company in the late 1970s.

Seen with their teacher, these children were all pupils of Catwg Primary School, Cadoxton, Neath in 1973.

Cam Gears automotive parts company employee Graham Williams setting a machine up at its Resolven plant, early 1990s.

Looking across Baglan towards Briton Ferry, from Mynydd Dinas, 2013. Baglan Primary School can be seen in the lower foreground.

A resident walks his dog along St Helier Drive, Sandfields, Port Talbot, 2007.

Excavators carve their way through the rock on the Earlswood side of the M4 Neath River crossing to allow for construction of the on-slip from the Swansea direction, 1993.

Members of Neath Boys' Grammar School's successful seven-a-side team, with teachers and a trophy they won during the 1958-1959 season.

The driver of this tractor would have been presented with an amazing panorama as he headed down Mynydd Dinas, Port Talbot after working in the fields at the top of the mountain in 2012.

Passengers wait on the platform at Neath General Station to board the 10.41train to Swansea, hauled by locomotive 4145, on May 9, 1953.

Holy Cross Church, Taibach surrounded by headstones in its graveyard after snowfall, 2013.

Some of the members of Y Gangen Sunday School, part of Jerusalem Chapel, Pontrhydyfen, mid-1950s.

Buses negotiate the busy Maypole corner junction of High Street and Water Street, Port Talbot alongside the Walnut Tree Hotel, while demolition work proceeds, early 1970s.

Head teacher Eric Lambourne with members of staff at Baglan Primary School, 1980.

Briton Ferry Road station, 1880. The scene behind will be familiar to many as the grounds of the Towers Hotel, Jersey Marine. The tower was originally built by Neath brewer Evan Evans in the late 1800s to house a camera obscura. He was the great-grandfather of Sir David Evans Bevan.

Locomotives 9796 and 3706 at Neath Riverside railway station prepare to haul the 11.25am train to Brecon on October 13, 1962.

Elizabeth (Betty) Catherine Morgan of Brynbryddan, Cwmavon and Gwyn Gower of Aberdare after their wedding at Goshen Chapel, The Graig, Cwmavon, on December 23, 1944. Betty celebrated her 90th birthday on May 30, 2016.

A bird's eye view of
Albion Works at
Briton Ferry
Steel Company,
November 17, 1978.

Members of Neath Boys' Grammar School's Tennis Team, 1964.

Heavy traffic at Station Road, Port Talbot, early 1950s. Just behind the buses is the level crossing of the Rhondda & Swansea Bay Railway line. The traffic chaos caused on this, the main A48 road from east to west across South Wales eventually resulted in construction of the M4 bypass around the town.

The impressive frontage of the Public Hall, Briton Ferry, early1960s belays the fact that its demolition was not too far away. A Tesco store currently occupies this site.

Members of Margam Senior Citizens Club during their annual dinner, 2007.

Three pupils of Neath Grammar School walk through the snow on Neath Abbey Road, 1978.

A police constable looks out from the M4 Neath River crossing towards BP Chemicals' Baglan Bay plant, shortly before the bridge opened to traffic on February 26, 1993.

Looking from its junction with Water Street at Maypole Corner, shoppers in High Street, Port Talbot, seem to be enjoying a particularly traffic free time, even for 1952.

A staff photo at Cwmafan Junior School with headteacher Wyndham Stone, centre front, 1952.

Neath Boys' Grammar School pupils who gained international honours, with one of their teachers, 1962.

The Plaza cinema, Talbot Road, Port Talbot, and right, shortly before their demolition, are the offices of the Port Talbot Railway & Dock Company, 2012.

A huge low loader transporter delivers some bulky equipment to the BP refinery at Llandarcy, during a significant expansion programme, early 1950s.

The wedding of Gwendoline Margaret Pollard and Donald Ridsdale at St Agnes Church, Forge Road, Port Talbot, March 30, 1957.

Some of the guests at the wedding of Robert and Thelma Mason, one of the first couples to be married at the Holy Trinity Church, Fairway, Sandfields, Port Talbot, August 20, 1966.

Neath Boys' Grammar School's Under 15 rugby squad, including three international caps, with their sports teacher, 1963.

The level crossing gates and signal box at Aberavon Town railway station, January 28, 1961. The town's Odeon cinema can be seen in the background.

The signal box and railway station at Cwmavon, May 13, 1954.

Betty Jones with her two daughters, Lynwen and Elaine on a shopping trip to Neath, 1950.

A group of Port Talbot Council painters, mid-1960s.

The Greyhound Public House, with Boots the Chemist alongside, Water Street, Neath, 1987.

Three Port Talbot recipients of Duke of Edinburgh Gold Awards and youth organisation representatives, 1967.

A group of railway enthusiasts at the western portal of the 1109 yard long Gyfylchi tunnel, near Tonmawr, following a landslip on May 29, 1954.

There was very much a country and western feel about this float, one of many which took part in Neath carnival, 1979.

Looking down on the Talbot Athletic ground, home to Aberavon RFC, September 8, 1996.

These five young Sandfields Comprehensive School pupils were Year 11 students who posed for a leaving photograph at the end of the summer term, 2004.

A tank engine at Briton Ferry railway yard, July 6, 1962.

It took a great deal of motive power in the early
1950s to haul this 130 ton de-asphalting tower to the
National Oil Refinery at Llandarcy. The equipment
was shipped into Swansea docks and hauled on the
last leg of its journey by vehicles of the Wynn's
heavy haulage company.

Crews of the Thomas Bros. bus
company sporting their new uniforms
in front of the Jersey Beach Hotel,
Aberavon seafront, 1936.

A 1978 panorama of Margam, Port Talbot steelworks and the town's tidal harbour.

Possibly the only pair of brothers from the Neath and Port Talbot area to serve in the Falklands War in 1982, Stephen Simons (front row with glasses) and Neil Simons on his right were given a civic reception by the Mayor of Port Talbot on their return. Stephen served on the submarine HMS Splendid and Neil served on HMS Herald, a survey vessel converted to floating hospital duties. Also included are the pair's proud parents and grandparents, together with the Mayor and Deputy Mayor.

Young and old came together for this gathering, attended by civic dignitaries at Sandfields Comprehensive School, mid-1970s.

The Coronation of Queen Elizabeth II in June 1953 was a special day for the residents of Tonmawr Road, Efail Fach, along with the rest of the nation. They held a street party outside number eight and were joined by people from nearby streets for the all-day celebration.

The point at which Neath Canal came to its end, near Rock House, Briton Ferry. Overlooking the spot are local authority homes built on Vernon Hill, 1952.

Andrew Hill, Gareth Cox and Adrian Hill with a medal gained after representing Port Talbot Sea Cadets at the national finals of a competition in Nottingham, 1998.

Members of the reception class at Glanymor Infant School, some dressed in traditional Welsh costume to celebrate St Davids Day 1980.

A group of railwaymen survey the results of a derailment of colliery wagons on the Incline at Ynysmaerdy, Briton Ferry.

Sandfields Comprehensive and Traethmelyn Schools, Port Talbot, 2011.

Crowds smile at the antics of two lively participants in the procession of Neath Carnival, 1979.

Steve Bowling and Huw Woodland in action during a Neath v Swansea rugby match, October 8, 1994.

Animal care workers taking a break at Margam Park's farm trail, 2006.

Cranes unload imported pit props for coal mines in the Afan Valley and beyond at Port Talbot Docks, 1946.

New Sandfields Association board members and volunteers at the Christmas dinner they held in the Four Winds Hotel, Aberavon Beach, December 2007.

Enthusiastic participants in Pontrhydyfen Junior
School's production of King Arthur, 1957.

Four young members of the Griffiths family
of Osborne Street, Neath, 1912.

David and Elizabeth Thomas of Cefn Don, formerly
Brook House, Llantwit Road, Neath, early 1900s.

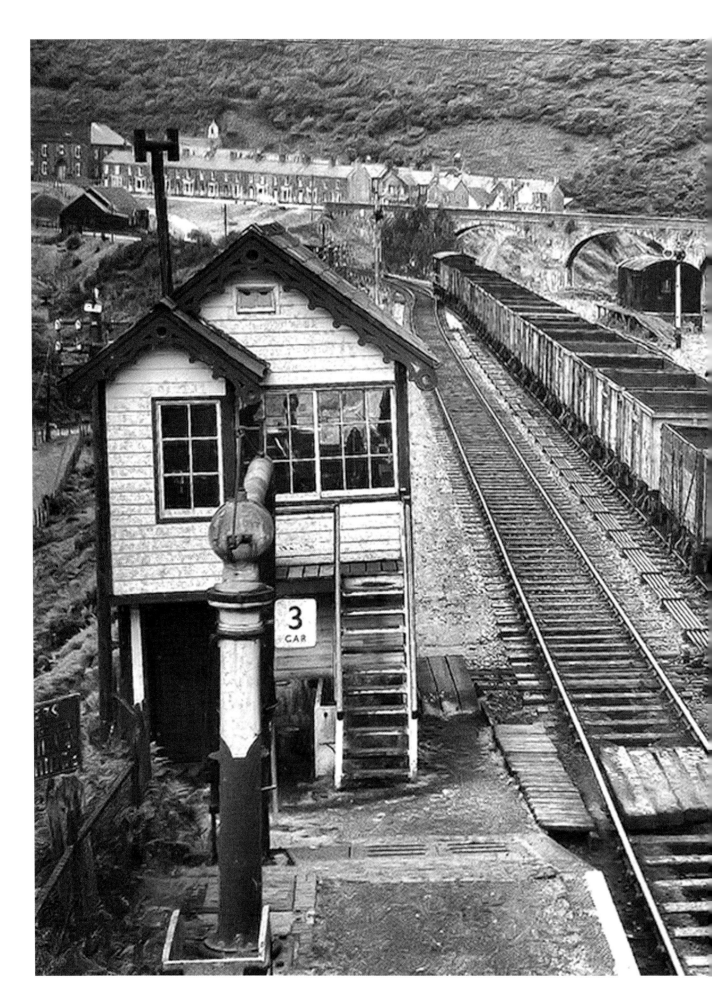

With Oakwood and nearby viaduct in the background a signalman at Pontrhydyfen Station and the driver of locomotive 9785 exchange the token that will allow it to proceed on its long haul up the Afan Valley with a trainload of empty coal wagons, August 22, 1962.

Commercial Road, Taibach, showing the rugby club and in the distance, the library, 1970s.

A group of pupils at Baglan Junior School, mid-1980s.

The rail link that served BP's Llandarcy oil refinery. With the refinery now gone, the site is being developed for housing and business use.

Some of the office staff and inspectors of Port Talbot's Thomas Bros. bus company, 1962.

Employees at Port Talbot's Iceland store in fancy dress, raising funds for charity, 2000.

This Welsh Water channel navigation buoy was washed up on Aberavon Beach in 2009.

A web of scaffolding greets the eye as construction work progresses on the slip road for the Earlswood M4 off-slip from the Neath River crossing, 1993.

Looking across Port Talbot towards St Mary's Church during demolition and redevelopment of the town, early 1970s. Though streets and properties have already disappeared, the roof of the town's market is still visible on the left along with some of the properties and industrial buildings that had long been a part of the town. In the foreground is Wern Chapel.

Members of the Orchard Place Baptist Church choir taking part in a Whitsun procession along Windsor Road, Neath, during the late 1950s.

Shops in New Road, Skewen, 1985.

Looking towards the castle ruins and the Moose Hall, Neath, during early town redevelopment, late 1970s.

Members of the 3rd Port Talbot Scout troop provided a unique guard of honour when this local couple emerged from their wedding at St Mary's Church, Aberavon, on June 16, 1962. The groom is Mr Harold Wilson, a holder of the Queen Scout award, and his bride, Miss Marlene Williams.

With Captain Jack Jones holding the ball this was Taibach RFC's successful team in the 1948-49 season interspersed with club officials.

Demolition work underway to allow for expansion of the South Wales Fork Truck company's headquarters at Crynant, Neath, 2003.

Margam Abbey after a dusting of snow, winter 1985.

Members of Orchard Place Baptist Church Youth Guild, Neath on a coach trip, 1956. The vehicle was supplied by Jenkins Coaches of Skewen.

A South Wales Transport Bristol VRT double decker waits outside the former Co-op food store at Alfred Street, Neath, before continuing on its next trip to Westernmoor, October 7, 1982.

Pupils of Dyffryn Grammar School taking part in an athletics competition during a sports day, late 1940s.

Choir girls of St Catharine's Church, Baglan, who dressed in Welsh costume at the request of a bride whose wedding they attended, 1967.

Machinery at work clearing silt from Cwm Clydach Pond, Dyffryn, Neath, September 1986.

Pupils from Catwg Primary School, Cadoxton, Neath, all dressed up for a Christmas concert.

A view of the rear of Baglan Hall, mid-1930s.

Neath Boys' Grammar School under 14 soccer team with their teacher and headteacher along with a trophy that hints at success in the 1962-63 season.

Ground clearance work before the building of new homes at Mariner's Point, Aberavon seafront, 1997.

The remains of the gatehouse to the Gnoll estate in Gnoll Avenue, Neath, 1983.

Ticket secretaries of Port Talbot Amateur Operatic Society, during its production of the musical Mame, 2000.

Looking down on Danybont, Pontrhydyfen, in the shadow of the village's landmark viaduct, 1970. Most of the trees in this view disappeared as part of a felling programme to eradicate a disease affecting particular species of evergreen trees.

Bus driver Bill James and conductress May Willie with her Bell Punch Ultimate ticket machine, mid 1950s.

Pupils of what was known as the Tin School, Cimla, Neath, 1957. It stood behind the town's fire station and served as an educational resource centre after being made redundant by the opening of Crynallt Primary School.

Cranes used for unloading imported coal and iron ore at Port Talbot Docks, before the opening of Port Talbot tidal harbour, late 1960s.

Neath Boys' Grammar School athletic team, with teachers, 1959.

Double deckers at the Cadoxton Road, Neath depot of the Western Welsh Omnibus Company Ltd. Opened in 1931, the bus garage was closed in July 1957, a short time after this scene was captured. It stood alongside the only engine shed of the Neath & Brecon Railway. It too closed in 1964.

Offices of the bus garage of the South Wales Transport bus company at Acacia Avenue, Sandfields, Port Talbot, December, 1987.

Guests at the official opening of the Steel Company of Wales works, Port Talbot, 1952.

Some of those who took part in a special charity walk across the M4 Neath River bridge shortly before it opened to traffic, 1993.

Just like this youngster, in 1991, generations of children have climbed aboard this former colliery tank locomotive that has been a landmark on the roadside at Cefn Coed Coal and Steam Museum, near Crynant, for many years.

The Ben Arron glass and decorators' materials shop was eventually one of the victims of demolition to make way for Port Talbot town centre redevelopment in the early 1970s. It was still serving townspeople when this picture was taken.

A view across the James Street redevelopment area on August 25, 1988 showing the offices of Watkins Bradfield accountants, later relocated at the other side of the scheme.

Foundation work underway in readiness for the building of what was originally Safeway's supermarket on the site of James Street, Neath, August 12, 1988.

The web of steel that supports the roof of Morrison's supermarket, Neath during town centre redevelopment, 1988. It was originally a Safeway store.

The Angel public house, Angel Street, Neath, 2006.

A class of pupils at Central Junior School, Port Talbot, in traditional Welsh costume on St David's Day, 1959.

There were some interesting guests at this Ascot Drive, Baglan, birthday party in 1979. From the right they are Richard Hughes, Martin Margetson, who became a Welsh soccer international, Crystal Palace stalwart and England goalkeeping coach; Michael Sheen, later an internationally acclaimed actor and Elaine Gower.

Pupils at Groes Primary School, Bertha Road, Margam, shortly after its official opening, July 10, 1973.

Talbot Square, sometimes referred to as Cwmavon Square, Port Talbot, 1973.

Neath Boys' Grammar School's athletic team, 1963 pictured with some of that year's trophies and the masters who spurred them on.

Mervyn and Kathleen Mayers with their daughter Barbara and son, Michael, during a visit to Neath Fair, 1948.

Employees of Power Gas, one of the contractors involved in the building of BP Chemicals' Baglan Bay Plant during a function at Baglan Social Club on May 18, 1971 to mark the end of their contract.

An interesting early 1950s bird's eye view of Port Talbot Docks that demonstrates its importance to the area's industries both for imports and exports during its heyday.

Houses alongside the River Afan at Carmarthen Row, Velindre, Port Talbot, shortly before they were demolished, late 1960s.

Shops at The Parade, Neath, February 11, 1990.

The Rhyddings Church schoolroom, Penywern Road, Neath, August, 1989.

Wisps of cloud fill the sky over the Jersey Beach Hotel, Aberavon, 1985.

Staff at the Cadoxton Road, Neath depot of the Western Welsh bus company take a break from their labours, early 1930s.

Members of the organising committee of the Port Talbot Scout group, late 1970s, during a visit from the town's Mayor.

An early 1900s view of the development of Aberavon Beach as a centre of seaside recreation, showing the Jersey Beach Hotel and beginnings of the promenade.

Members of Neath Boys' Grammar School's 1st cricket XI, with the school's head teacher and teachers 1963.

Members of the male chorus of the Melyncrythan Amateur Operatic Society's production of the musical, The White Horse Inn, 1958.

Choristers of Pelenna Valley Choir, with musical director Sid Jones and accompanist Vicky Dummer, 1980.

Some of those who took part in the street party held to celebrate the Investiture of the Prince of Wales, at Upper West End, Taibach, Port Talbot, July 1969.

Women of Salem Chapel, Sandfields, Port Talbot, with Mayor, Councillor Margaret Victory, during a visit to the Mayor's parlour, 1979.

Members of Afan Borough Council's
environmental committee during an inspection
tour of BP Chemicals' Baglan Bay plant, 1975.

Looking towards Neath shortly before the
opening of the town's Northern Link Road
bridge. Work is underway alongside on
what was initially Safeway, and became
Morrison's supermarket, mid-1980s.

Blodwyn and Joe Morgan outside Graig Apostolic Chapel, Cwmavon, early 1950s. Joe was a deacon of the chapel for more than 50 years.

A group of cricketers who played for the Orchard Place Baptist Church side, 1958.

Bryn Cottage, Coed Parc, Cwmavon. Once owned by a local baker it was demolished in the late 1960s.

Properties at the junction of High Street and Old Market Street, Neath, which were demolished shortly after this in 1972. The Iceland supermarket store is here now.

A gathering at the Avondale Hotel, High Street, Port Talbot, 1972.

A South Sea Islands performance that formed part of a 1980s Scout and Guide Neath Gang Show at Neath.

Unusual motive power hauls a mixed freight train passing through Port Talbot General Station with the now vanished Margam Terrace alongside, on April 13, 1962.

A young Ray Bruten on his horse Royal at Penstar Farm, Pontrhydyfen, 1950.

Demolition of premises at the junction of Old Market Street, adjoining the Duke of Wellington public house, March 1973.

The Railway Inn, Bridge Street,
Neath, 1984.

The ornate bandstand at
Victoria Gardens, Neath, a popular
gathering point, summer 2008.

Two of the participants in the Passion
Play performance staged at Margam
Park, in the 1980s.

New Hunter Street, Briton Ferry, 1920s.

Participants, many of them youngsters, prepare for a Whitsun parade at Taibach, Port Talbot, 1956.

A proud dad takes his baby daughter for a Sunday morning stroll at Brynna Road, Cwmavon, 1970.

Ian Boobyer in action for Neath RFC during their game against Newport on March 30, 1996.

Commercial premises in The Parade, Neath, February 1990.

Ty Afan school, Pendarvis Terrace, Port Talbot, before demolition, 2012.

The final days of the former overhead railway bridge that became known as the Beach Hill, 2006.

Construction of Briton Ferry Viaduct early 1950s. Work began in 1949 and together with Neath River bridge it was opened to traffic in October 1955.

Construction of the M4 flyover and Pentyla slip road, September,1965.

St. Catharine's Church
Baglan, mid-1930s.

A cheery faced group of pupils who attended the Gnoll Boys' Junior School, 1949.

Davies Builders Merchants, Green Park Industrial Estate, Port Talbot, before the company relocated to Endeavour Close, Sandfields, and the old site was demolished to make way for housing, 2012.

A unique aerial
view of works
at Briton Ferry,
1929 showing
Vernon House
on the hill
overlooking
Briton Ferry
Dock and the
Whitford Pond
which provided
cooling water
for the works.

A class of pupils at Baglan Junior School, with their teacher Mr Overton, late 1960s.

Some of the cast members of the play Jam for Mrs Heggie, that was staged by members of the Young Wives group of St Michael's Church, Cwmavon.

The Mission Hall, High Street, Neath, November 1974.

Pupils at Tirmorfa Infants School, Sandfields, Port Talbot, on St David's day, 1968.

Properties in Neath Road, Briton Ferry, 1920s.

The overhead railway bridge that spanned the lower end of Villiers Street, Briton Ferry. It carried the Rhondda & Swansea Bay Railway and was demolished in 1936.

Members of the maintenance crew of Nos. 4 and 5 blast furnaces at the British Steel Corporation's Port Talbot steelworks, mid-1980s.

Children of Gladys Street, Aberavon, late 1940s. They certainly seem to have been prepared for the photographer!

Looking towards the Oxford Inn from Briton Ferry Road, Neath, at Stockham's Corner, 1988.

The Neath and Brecon public house, Bridge Street, Neath, shortly before its demolition along with neighbouring properties, 1982.

Headteacher Mr JV Davies with staff at Dyffryn Comprehensive Upper School, Margam, Port Talbot, 1970.

Demolition of Customs House, Talbot Road, Port Talbot, in progress, 2012.

Members of the congregation of Orchard Place Baptist Church, Neath, in the town's Windsor Road, during its Whitsun procession, 1960.

The Masonic Hall, Water Street, Neath, March 1971.

Thomas Bros. (Port Talbot) Ltd, added these three 36ft long AEC Reliance 470 buses to its fleet of 41 vehicles in 1963. The vehicles were unusual in having illuminated advertisement panels. The company was taken over by the South Wales Transport Company in 1971.

Looking across Neath from
Drummau Mountain, 1985.

With the telephone exchange in the background, a Swansea-bound bus heads along Prince of Wales Drive, Neath, on October 7, 1982.

A snowbound Southdown View, Sandfields, Port Talbot, March 2009.

Stores including that of FW
Woolworth, in Church Street,
Port Talbot, late 1960s.

The country's biggest post Second World War civil engineering project for many years was the construction of Neath River bridge at Briton Ferry. It is seen here towering over boats moored near the Monkstone Cruising and Sailing Club, while the Wern aluminium works can be seen in the background, late 1960s.

Snow covers the playing fields alongside the now demolished Sandfields Youth Centre, Seaway Parade, 2009.

Kiwis public House, at the junction of the The Parade and The Croft, Neath, 2006. It was previously known as The Harrier.

Pupils at Cwmavon Primary School, during St David's Day, 1977.

A class at Tonmawr Infants School with their teacher and headteacher 1949.

Looking seawards from the M4 bridge
across the River Neath with the
Monkstone Cruising and Sailing Club
marina in the foreground, late 1990s.

Close inspection reveals that much has changed since this bird's eye view of Neath was captured in 1964.

Representatives of St Mary's Church, Port Talbot, mid-1970s during a presentation.

The view towards the pulpit across the interior of Dyffryn Chapel, Taibach, Port Talbot, which closed in 1997.

A class at Tonmawr Junior School with their teacher and headteacher, 1949.

A proud mum and grandmother with young babies Elaine and Lynn Gower, outside the Apostolic Church at Brynna Road, Cwmavon, shortly before their dedication, 1972.

Looking along the railway from New Road, Jersey Marine, towards the former EM Edwards gas works, 1973.

Caravan homes at the traveller camp, Briton Ferry, late 1990s.

Members of three generations of the Hughes and Edwards families gather together at Brynbryddan, Cwmavon, during the summer of 1947.

The tank engine Eileen shunting coal trucks at Duffryn Rhondda Colliery in the Afan Valley on July 11,1968. Part of the village of Abercregan, most of the terraces of which have now been demolished, can be seen in the background.

Wind Street, Neath, June 1977, with three businesses which have long since vanished.

Looking along Duck Street, Neath, towards New Street, March 1971.

Guests at the official opening of the Steel Company of Wales, Port Talbot, July 17, 1951.

Members of Taibach youth rugby team, with club officials, 1950.

Youngsters
Philip and
Gaynor
Mayers at
Brynderwen
House,
Drummau,
Skewen,
1960.

Pupils of Class 3, Eastern Infants School, Taibach, seen with their teacher, September 1924.

A view across the rooftops of Briton Ferry, early 1950s.

The Greyhound public house, Water Street, Neath, stands alone after buildings either side had been demolished to provide access for the building of the town's Boots the Chemists store, early 1980s.

Properties in Talbot Road, Port Talbot, including the YMCA, February 11, 1987.

The Kings Arms, Windsor Road, Neath, July 1976.

Cast members of a pantomime staged by members of Taibach Rugby Club, late 1970s.

A group of blast furnacemen at Port Talbot steelworks during a retirement presentation to one of their colleagues, November 1996.

Construction work on the Port Talbot distributor road near the former Beach Hill bridge, 2008.

The former Hospital for Souls, at Water Street, Neath, shortly before the building was demolished, 1969.

Pupils of Pencaerau Secondary School, Neath, with headmaster Mr Williams and teachers, 1956.

Pupils of form 1B Glanafan School, Port Talbot, 1972.

The 9.30am Treherbert to Swansea train hauled by locomotive 3685 passes through Aberavon Town station and Port Talbot (Aberavon Town) signal box on August 21, 1962.

Staff of the British Steel Corporation's Port Talbot works and partners at their Christmas party, 1977.

Passengers alight from a train heading for Neath Riverside station at Glynneath, May 30, 1964.

Looking up the magnificent cascades at the Gnoll Park, Neath, July, 2013. They were originally created by Sir Humphrey Mackworth during 1730 when he extended the Gnoll House.

Houses under construction at Ascot Drive, Baglan, 1972.

Boarded up properties awaiting demolition, made Bridge Street, Neath, a sad looking location, 1988.

Residents of Mozart Court residential home, Sandfields, Port Talbot, on St David's Day, 1984.

The view from the hillside overlooking BP Chemicals' Baglan Bay plant, 1983.

Employees gather to witness the last tap of K Furnace at the Briton Ferry Steel Company, November 17, 1978.

Looking seaward across a much silted-up Briton Ferry Dock towards the River Neath estuary, 1994.

Four generations of the Morgan family of Wood Street, Taibach, 1948. Right to left included are 'Mam' Morgan, Joe Morgan, Elizabeth Gower nee Morgan and Hadrian Gower.

A teacher proudly stands alongside her class of pupils at Catwg Primary School, 1977.

Members of Wern Congregational Chapel, Aberavon, take part in a Whitsun procession, early 1950s.

Many of the nurses in this group who received their certificates from HRH the Prince of Wales, at the Brangwyn Hall, Swansea, December 1977, were residents of Neath and Port Talbot.

The approach to the 167 yard
long Pontrhydyfen Viaduct
between Tonmawr and
Aberavon Junction, 1962.

Snow covered rooftops of the Central Primary School and surrounding properties, looking towards Talbot Road, Port Talbot, 1984.

This group of women entered the Briton Ferry Pram Parade as the aerobic girls, 1989.

Shops at Stockham's Corner, Neath, looking into Windsor Road, early 1970s.

The official opening of Fairway Co-operative Store, Sandfields, Port Talbot, 1957.

Skewen Salvation Army
Corps Census Board,
March, 1972.

Pupils at Central
Junior School,
Port Talbot, 1958.

190

The M4 makes its snake like progress across Port Talbot during the final stages of construction, May 1966.

A Western Welsh bus company fitter stands alongside an AEC Regal vehicle at the company's Cadoxton Road, Neath depot, mid-1930s.

St David's Church viewed across
Victoria Gardens, Neath, summer 2008.